SCIENCE AND TECHNOLOGY

in the Twenty-First Century

by Elisabeth Herschbach

ReferencePoint
Press®

San Diego, CA

© 2020 ReferencePoint Press, Inc.
Printed in the United States

For more information, contact:
ReferencePoint Press, Inc.
PO Box 27779
San Diego, CA 92198
www.ReferencePointPress.com

LIBRARY OF CONGRESS CATALOGING-IN-PUBLICATION DATA

Name: Herschbach, Elisabeth, 1972– author.
Title: Science and Technology in the Twenty-First Century/by Elisabeth Herschbach.
Description: San Diego, CA: ReferencePoint Press, Inc., [2020] | Series: Defining Events of
the Twenty-First Century | Audience: Grade 9 to 12 | Includes bibliographical references and
index.
ISBN: 978-1-68282-605-8 (hardback)
ISBN: 978-1-68282-606-5 (ebook)
The complete Library of Congress record is available at www.loc.gov.

CONTENTS

IMPORTANT EVENTS

2003
The Human Genome Project is completed, mapping out the full human genetic blueprint and paving the way for new lifesaving treatments.

2012
Curiosity, the most ambitious robotic rover ever sent to another planet, lands on Mars to search for evidence of past life.

2012
Scientists develop a new gene-editing technique known as CRISPR, allowing researchers to target very specific regions of the genome more cheaply, easily, and precisely.

2007
Tech company Apple releases the first iPhone and jumpstarts a new era of mobile computing that changes how people connect and communicate.

2009
The Kepler space telescope launches on a nine-year mission to search for planets beyond our solar system.

| 2003 | 2006 | 2009 | 2012 |

2006
The popular social networking site Facebook opens for general registration, fueling a social media explosion.

2009
Google begins developing and testing self-driving vehicles.

2015

NASA's *New Horizons* spacecraft makes a historic flyby of Pluto.

2017

Researchers at Newcastle University in the United Kingdom test a bionic hand controlled by a computer vision system that learns to recognize objects.

2016

The Laser Interferometer Gravitational Wave Observatory (LIGO) detects gravitational waves for the first time ever, confirming part of Einstein's theory of relativity.

2018

The Transiting Exoplanet Survey Satellite (TESS) launches, continuing Kepler's mission of searching for exoplanets.

2015   2018   2021

2015

For the first time ever, doctors successfully treat a leukemia patient with genetically engineered immune cells from a donor.

2019

New Horizons flies by Kuiper Belt object 2014 MU69 on New Year's Day.

2017

Stanford University researchers develop an artificial intelligence system for detecting skin cancer.

A Journey of Discovery

On February 24, 2011, the space shuttle *Discovery* stood on the launch pad at the Kennedy Space Center in Florida, ready for its final mission. Parked cars lined the roads leading to the launch site, and eager spectators thronged nearby beaches, angling for a good view. At the Kennedy Space Center, a crowd of roughly 40,000 waited in anticipation.

Before boarding the airliner-sized orbiter, Commander Steven Lindsey and his crew of five other astronauts joined in a group hug at the base of the launch pad. "Enjoy the ride," the test conductor radioed to them.[1] A last-minute computer glitch stalled the countdown for a few minutes, keeping spectators in suspense. Then, with just seconds to spare before the launch deadline closed, the powerful machine thundered into the air. "*Discovery* now making one last reach for the stars," the Mission Control announcer proclaimed as the spacecraft traced a fiery arc in the cloudless blue sky.[2]

The launch was historic because it was the concluding mission of the world's longest-serving space shuttle, marking the beginning of the end of an era. In August 2011, the US National Aeronautics and Space Administration (NASA) formally closed down the whole space

The space shuttle *Discovery* lifted off on its final mission on the afternoon of February 24, 2011. It was the shuttle's thirty-ninth mission.

shuttle program. But *Discovery*'s last journey also represented a more positive milestone for space exploration: the completion of the final main section of the International Space Station (ISS). *Discovery* was on its way to deliver a new module to the orbiting laboratory, wrapping up a construction job that began in 1998 and took thirteen years to finish.

A Marvel of Engineering— and International Teamwork

Home to visiting crews of astronauts and scientists, the ISS orbits at an average altitude of approximately 248 miles (400 km) above Earth, zooming around the planet every ninety minutes at about 17,500 miles per hour (28,000 km/h). The football field–sized space station is the most ambitious, most expensive, and largest structure ever put in space. Each section—built out of tens of thousands of components—had to be launched separately and assembled in orbit. "I don't think it's overstating it to say it's the greatest technological achievement that humans have gotten to at this point," says NASA astronaut Tom Marshburn, who lived and worked on the ISS in 2012 and 2013.[3]

The ISS is not just an achievement in science and engineering. It also represents a remarkable feat of global cooperation. "It's been a great model for countries to come together to work alongside each other, to understand each other and launch out to the planets together," says former NASA engineer David Baker.[4] Building the 100-billion-dollar project took work by fifteen different nations. And by 2018, more than 230 people from eighteen different countries have visited the space station, collaborating on hundreds of research projects. "I was constantly astounded by what human beings from around the world had accomplished," Marshburn says. "It's just a dream come true in a lot of ways."[5]

Intersecting Innovations

The ISS is a powerful symbol of how the spirit of exploration can spur discoveries in many intersecting areas of science. That same dynamic is also behind many other important innovations in twenty-first-century science and technology.

Innovations in artificial intelligence and computing have given today's medical researchers unprecedented insights into the human genetic code. With powerful new bioengineering tools, doctors are finding ways to alter the DNA in human cells to cure diseases and even reprogram our biology. Meanwhile, advances in computing have also ushered in new telecommunications technologies, changing how the web works and how we use it. High-speed internet connections and smartphones are changing how we communicate and interact with others. At the same time, these telecommunications tools have inspired a new generation of connected technologies that are revamping our homes and workplaces. Innovative applications are even being put to use to improve health care.

Robotics research is fueling breakthroughs in the design of self-driving cars and other autonomous machines. These same advances in robotics are also revolutionizing medical devices such as prostheses, helping many people overcome disabilities. And they are helping space scientists expand the horizons of space exploration and research. Robotic rovers on Mars and elsewhere are changing what we know about our solar system and the universe beyond. And robots are facilitating the pioneering work of astronauts. For example, when the space shuttle *Discovery* made its historic final delivery to the ISS, a state-of-the-art robotic arm developed by Canadian robotics firm MDA unloaded and attached the cargo to the orbiting station.

"One of the defining characteristics of our species is its drive to discover, to constantly push the boundaries of what is known and what is possible," say biochemists Jennifer Doudna and Samuel Sternberg.[6] That drive to push boundaries is fueling new discoveries and new innovations in science and technology that are transforming human knowledge and human experience in the twenty-first century and beyond.

> **"One of the defining characteristics of our species is its drive to discover, to constantly push the boundaries of what is known and what is possible."[6]**
>
> *– Biochemists Jennifer Doudna and Samuel Sternberg*

Chapter 1

What Breakthroughs Are Happening in Space Science?

On the morning of February 11, 2016, physicist David Reitze, executive director of the Laser Interferometer Gravitational Wave Observatory (LIGO), stood at the podium in front of a packed room at the National Press Club in Washington, DC. "Ladies and gentlemen, we have detected gravitational waves," a grinning Reitze announced. "We did it!"[7] The room erupted in cheers and applause. So did university auditoriums across the nation, where excited students and professors gathered to watch the live-streamed press conference.

Scientists around the world hailed the event as a historic first, one of the most important breakthroughs in the history of space science. Researchers Rainer Weiss, Kip Thorne, and Barry Barish, the masterminds behind LIGO, won the 2017 Nobel Prize in Physics for the achievement. The Royal Swedish Academy of Sciences, which awards the prizes, called it "a discovery that shook the world."[8]

Catching the Wave

Gravitational waves are ripples or distortions in space-time first predicted by Albert Einstein in his 1916 theory of relativity. According

Researcher Kip Thorne spoke to the media about the gravitational wave discovery in 2016. The existence of this phenomenon had been predicted a century earlier.

to Einstein's theory, objects moving through the universe warp or bend the fabric of time and space—much the way that a heavy ball thrown into an outstretched blanket will curve the blanket downward. That warping of space-time is what we experience as gravity.

The space-time distortions created by very massive objects like neutron stars and black holes, Einstein predicted, should ripple across the universe and theoretically be measurable by scientists. Yet long after Einstein first published his theory, the detection of these gravitational waves continued to elude scientists—until LIGO's breakthrough a century later.

Operated jointly by the Massachusetts Institute of Technology (MIT) and the California Institute of Technology (CalTech), LIGO consists of two gigantic interferometers. These are powerful devices that use lasers and mirrors to measure patterns of interference from beams of light. These ultraprecise detectors are capable of measuring tiny fluctuations made by gravitational waves—changes in space-time thousands of times smaller than an atom's nucleus. It's "the most sensitive instrument ever built," according to Reitze.[9]

That precision paid off. On September 14, 2015, LIGO scientists picked up a signal. Lengthy statistical tests over the next several months confirmed that scientists had recorded the stretching and warping of space-time from two black holes, the gravitational fields left behind when very massive stars collapse. It was the scientific community's first detection of binary black holes: two black holes spiraling together in close orbit. As the massive pair collided and merged into an even larger black hole sixty-two times the mass of the Sun, the collision released energy in the form of gravitational waves—ripples in space-time lasting mere milliseconds. "The signal took a billion years to come to Earth and produce this tiny distortion in our detectors that we are very proud to measure," says LIGO spokesperson Gabriela González, a Louisiana State University professor of physics and astronomy.[10]

A New Window on the Universe

The detection of gravitational waves not only validates Einstein's predictions but also gives scientists today new tools for exploring the universe. "Detecting and analyzing the information carried by gravitational waves is allowing us to observe the universe in a way never before possible," LIGO team members explain in an online statement. "With this completely new way of examining astrophysical objects and phenomena, LIGO has opened a new window on the universe."[11]

Unlike light waves, which can be blocked or distorted by matter, gravitational waves travel through space unaltered. This means that scientists may potentially be able to examine realms of space—such as black holes—that up to now have been unobservable because they give off no visible light. "It's like Galileo pointing the telescope for the first time at the sky," says Vassiliki Kalogera, a professor of physics and astronomy at Northwestern University. "You're opening your eyes—in this case, our ears—to a new set of signals from the universe that our previous technologies did not allow us to receive, study, and learn from."[12] Some scientists even think that gravitational waves may eventually make it possible to study the Big Bang itself, providing insight into the universe's beginnings some 13.8 billion years ago, when conditions were too hot and dense for any light to be dispersed. In the meantime, gravitational wave research is already producing groundbreaking results.

In August 2017, LIGO and its sister observatory Virgo, based in Italy, jointly recorded gravitational waves traced to a pair of colliding neutron stars, the collapsed cores of exploded stars. These densely packed dead stars crashed into each other and merged 130 million light-years away, sparking an electromagnetic burst called a kilonova. Thanks to the signals picked

> **"Detecting and analyzing the information carried by gravitational waves is allowing us to observe the universe in a way never before possible."[11]**
>
> *– LIGO team members in an online statement*

up by LIGO and Virgo, astronomers were able to pinpoint where to look in the sky, witnessing the fiery explosion as it unfolded. This was the first time scientists were able to use gravitational waves to locate an object or event in space. It was also the first time scientists had ever observed two neutron stars merging.

Kepler and the Search for Exoplanets

LIGO's detection of gravitational waves wowed the science world by finally confirming a century-old idea from Einstein. Other twenty-first-century advances in space science have made history by discovering results never before predicted. One of these trailblazers was the Kepler spacecraft, launched by NASA in 2009.

Named after seventeenth-century astronomer Johannes Kepler, the high-tech space telescope orbited in deep space for nine years, searching for exoplanets—planets outside of our solar system. In the process, the Kepler mission overturned many previous assumptions about the nature of planets and solar systems, transforming our understanding of the universe and our place in it. "It's probably the one mission that's changed the history of humankind more than any other," says mission founder William Borucki, who was a space scientist at NASA's Ames Research Center until his retirement in 2015.[13]

Outfitted with the largest camera ever launched into space, Kepler blasted off from Cape Canaveral, Florida, on March 7, 2009. Circling the sun at a distance of more than 90 million miles (145 million km) from Earth, the 2,300-pound (1,040-kg) spacecraft hunted for exoplanets using a strategy known as the transit method. This involves precisely measuring the brightness of stars, looking for slight dimmings of light that may indicate an orbiting planet passing—or

Technicians built the Kepler spacecraft in a tightly controlled clean room to keep it in perfect condition. The spacecraft would go on to make important discoveries in planetary science.

transiting—in front of a star. By carefully analyzing such patterns of starlight, scientists can infer not just the existence of a planet, but also its size, distance from its parent star, and length of orbit. During its nine-year mission, Kepler monitored more than half a million stars, some up to 3,000 light-years away, watching for telltale dips in starlight. By the time the spacecraft ran out of fuel in 2018, it had discovered more than 2,600 confirmed exoplanets. Almost 3,000 more candidate planets identified by Kepler still awaited confirmation.

Before the launch of Kepler, scientists knew very little about planets beyond our solar system. A few large, Jupiter-sized exoplanets had previously been detected by astronomers, but scientists were still largely in the dark about what smaller worlds might be orbiting other suns. Kepler changed that. As NASA's first planet-hunting mission, Kepler gave researchers an unprecedented trove of data to study. And the results showed that planets are more prevalent throughout the galaxy than scientists had expected—and far more diverse.

The Goldilocks Zone

Scientists still have many unanswered questions about exoplanets and distant solar systems, but Kepler has been a game-changer. "To say Kepler revolutionized our understanding of the cosmos is no overstatement," science writer Nadia Drake puts it.[14] Kepler's most important legacy is the discovery of potentially Earth-like planets beyond our solar system. Kepler was the first mission to identify Earth-sized rocky planets orbiting in what scientists call the Goldilocks, or habitable, zone of their stars. This is the region around a star where temperatures are neither too hot nor too cold for the planet to have liquid water on its surface. Liquid water is thought to be a requirement for life.

> **"To say Kepler revolutionized our understanding of the cosmos is no overstatement."[14]**
>
> *—Science writer Nadia Drake*

Thanks to Kepler, scientists now know that potentially habitable planets are relatively common throughout the galaxy. Extrapolating from the data Kepler collected, researchers calculate that some 20 to 50 percent of the billions of stars in the Milky Way are likely to have small rocky planets in their habitable zones. This is a significant finding because it takes us one step closer to discovering life on other planets. "It's time to search

Life on Mars?

Being the right distance from a star is not enough to make a planet habitable. Other factors, including the planet's size and atmosphere, are also crucial. In our solar system, Mars's distance from the sun puts it just at the edge of the Goldilocks zone. Its size makes it the most similar to Earth of all the other planets in our solar system. Yet today the planet is dry and barren. That's because its thin atmosphere allows in too much radiation from the sun, making the environment unsuitable for life.

Were the environmental conditions on Mars ever different? Could Earth's neighbor once have been habitable? Thanks to data collected by the Mars rover *Curiosity*, scientists now think the answer is yes. The largest rover ever launched to another planet, the car-sized mobile laboratory touched down on Mars in August 2012. *Curiosity* is NASA's most ambitious Mars mission to date. Equipped with numerous scientific instruments, including a robotic arm, cameras, and sophisticated measurement tools, it analyzes features of the planet's environment for clues into its past. Intriguingly, the rover has detected a variety of organic molecules in rock samples, thought to be among the chemical ingredients for carbon-based life. It has also found signs of an ancient streambed, indicating that the planet likely had flowing water in the past. Scientists now think Mars once had the conditions necessary for supporting microbial life.

the habitable zones of nearby stars to find our nearest neighbors," says Courtney Dressing, a professor of astronomy at the University of California, Berkeley.[15]

Although Kepler was retired by NASA in 2018, its discoveries have set the agenda for decades of future research in astronomy. New missions are poised to build on Kepler's successes. NASA's Transiting Exoplanet Survey Satellite (TESS), launched in 2018, is searching for exoplanets using the transit method in an area 400 times larger than

Kepler's range. Scanning 85 percent of the sky, TESS will focus on the brightest, closest stars in the Milky Way system. The goal is to identify the most promising planets for follow-up study by other space observatories and ground-based telescopes.

The James Webb Space Telescope, a collaboration between NASA, the European Space Agency (ESA), and the Canadian Space Agency, will study the atmospheres of exoplanets, searching for signs of the chemical components needed to sustain life. Scheduled to launch in March 2021, the giant infrared telescope boasts a tennis court–sized solar shield that will block light from the sun so that scientists can get an unobscured view of distant planets.

New Horizons: Pluto Up Close

While the Kepler space telescope helped to bring the far reaches of the galaxy into better view, NASA's *New Horizons* mission took scientists into uncharted territory closer to home. On July 14, 2015, the unmanned robotic spacecraft made headlines by carrying out the first mission to Pluto, taking the first high-resolution images of the remote, icy dwarf planet at the edge of the solar system. With this achievement, NASA finally completed the last milestone in a fifty-year quest to tour the solar system that began with the *Mariner 4* Mars mission in 1964. "It turned the last of the planets known at the birth of the Space Age from a faraway point of light into a real place that humans have now come to know," say planetary scientists Alan Stern and David Grinspoon in their book *Chasing New Horizons*.[16]

At the same time, *New Horizons* also opened a new chapter in space exploration, becoming the first spacecraft to explore the Kuiper Belt, a little-understood region of rocky and icy objects past Neptune. The trillions of frozen worlds in this region are thought to be leftover debris from the cloud of gas, dust, and rocks that pulled together to form the solar system some 4.6 billion years ago. As the largest object in the Kuiper Belt, Pluto may be a gateway to better understanding how our solar system formed and evolved, scientists say.

Launched in January 2006, *New Horizons* hurtled away from Earth at more than 36,000 miles per hour (58,000 km/h), setting a record for the fastest-ever recorded spacecraft speed at launch. "We built the smallest spacecraft we could get away with that has all the things it needs . . . and put it on the biggest possible launch vehicle," Stern says. "That combination was ferocious in terms of the speed we reached in deep space."[17]

In just nine hours, the roughly grand piano–sized probe reached the moon—a distance that took the Apollo astronauts three days. In thirteen months, the spacecraft reached Jupiter, some 500 million miles (800 million km) away. From there, *New Horizons* boosted its speed to a blazing 52,000 miles per hour (83,600 km/h), taking advantage of a gravity assist from Jupiter. This is a technique that allows a spacecraft to harness a planet's gravity to change its speed and direction on its way to its next target.

Without the gravity assist from Jupiter, *New Horizons* would have needed fourteen years to get to Pluto. Instead, the 3-billion-mile (4.8-billion-km) journey took just nine and a half years. At such great

> **"We built the smallest spacecraft we could get away with that has all the things it needs . . . and put it on the biggest possible launch vehicle. That combination was ferocious in terms of the speed we reached in deep space."[17]**
>
> *– Planetary scientist Alan Stern, on the space probe's journey to Pluto*

speeds, however, it was impossible for the lightweight probe to slow down and go into orbit around Pluto or to land. As a result, *New Horizons* was designed to be a flyby mission, snapping pictures and gathering data about the dwarf planet and its moons as the spacecraft zoomed by. Even that was an astoundingly challenging feat to pull off.

Mission scientists calculated that *New Horizons* had to maintain a distance of 7,800 miles (12,600 km) from Pluto for the best images. Any closer would yield blurry pictures because of the spacecraft's speed; farther away would mean not enough detail. To pull off the desired precision, the spacecraft could be no more than 60 miles (100 km) off course at the time of its closest approach. "This was the equivalent of hitting a golf ball from L.A. to New York and landing it in a target the size of a soup can," Stern and Grinspoon quip.[18]

An Incredible Voyage

Early in the morning on July 14, 2015, *New Horizons* team members waited anxiously at the Mission Operations Center in the Applied Physics Laboratory in Laurel, Maryland. The long-anticipated flyby day had come. *New Horizons* was due to make its closest approach to Pluto at 7:50 am. Crowds of staff members, journalists, and other guests waved flags and cheered as giant countdown clocks flashed the time.

Despite the festive atmosphere, there was an undercurrent of nervousness rippling through the room. *New Horizons* hadn't transmitted any signs of life for more than twenty hours. As planned, communications with the spacecraft had been shut down as it approached Pluto. This was to conserve power for collecting the maximum number of close-up photos and scans.

New Horizons captured incredible photos of Pluto. Scientists got their first-ever close-up views of the mysterious dwarf planet.

Confirmation of the successful flyby didn't come until that evening. At 8:53 pm, the check-in signal finally arrived. Mission operations manager Alice Bowman tensely scanned pages of status reports beamed in from the spacecraft, already speeding away from Pluto. "We have a healthy spacecraft, we have collected all the data, and we are outbound from Pluto," she announced at last.[19] Team members beamed with joy, exchanging hugs, handshakes, and high-fives.

Reduce, Reuse, Recycle

New Horizons blasted into space on an Atlas V rocket, one of NASA's most powerful rockets. A Delta II rocket propelled the Kepler telescope into space. These rockets are impressive powerhouses, but they are costly—and wasteful. That's because they are expendable rockets, designed for one-time use. After liftoff, the first stage of the rocket separates off and falls back to Earth, sinking into the ocean, never to be used again. For every new launch, an entirely new rocket and engines have to be built from scratch.

Until 2015, no rockets were capable of making it to space and then landing intact back on Earth. Entrepreneurs like SpaceX founder Elon Musk and Amazon CEO Jeff Bezos have been working to usher in a new age of reusable rockets. In November 2015, Bezos's private spaceflight company Blue Origin made history by launching the first rocket to reach space and then land successfully. Shortly afterwards, Musk's Falcon 9 rocket became the first to land intact after launching a mission into orbit. Reusable rockets have been hailed as the next crucial advance in space exploration, with the potential to dramatically lower the costs of space exploration. Both Bezos and Musk have the long-term goal of transporting passengers to space.

A Scientific Wonderland

It took fifteen months for *New Horizons* to send all the data it collected back home, but as soon as the first signals started trickling in, NASA scientists knew that all the hype was well deserved. "It's the stuff of history," Stern says. "We're seeing that Pluto is a scientific wonderland."[20]

New Horizons' sophisticated cameras and on-board instruments captured stunningly detailed images and scans that allowed scientists to map Pluto's surface for the first time and study the rocks, ices, and gases that make up its landscape and atmosphere. The close-up images and scans revealed a strikingly diverse and complex world with deep craters, towering ice mountains, vast plains of frozen methane and nitrogen ice, suspected ice volcanoes, and even possible evidence of an underground liquid ocean under its icy crust.

This complexity surpassed anything scientists expected to find on the distant, frozen world, forcing a rethinking of some long-held assumptions in planetary science. Following conventional scientific wisdom, researchers expected Pluto to be geologically dead, lacking the heat sources that cause tectonic plates to shift, shaping and reshaping landforms. Yet evidence from *New Horizons* tells a different story. In some places, Pluto's surface appears to be ancient and heavily cratered; in others, it has the smooth, crater-free appearance of younger land formations. This is an intriguing sign that the 4.5-billion-year-old dwarf planet may still be very much geologically alive.

Beyond Pluto

New Horizons' odyssey is not over. After speeding past Pluto, the pioneering probe continued its journey deeper into the Kuiper Belt. On January 1, 2019, it made another epic flyby mission. This time its target was 2014 MU69, a small Kuiper Belt object 1 billion miles (1.6 billion km) beyond Pluto and 4 billion miles (6.6 billion km) from Earth.

Scientists say reaching it was like traveling 4.5 billion years into the past. Because so little sun reaches this part of the solar system, scientists think that MU69 and other objects orbiting in this region are like time capsules from the dawn of the solar system, preserved virtually unchanged in a deep freeze for billions of years. "Going to it is like making an archaeological dig into the history of our solar system," Stern says.[21]

Chapter 2

How Has Technology Changed the Way We Communicate?

Following its landing on Mars in 2012, the NASA rover *Curiosity* used ten state-of-the-art scientific instruments and seventeen cameras to collect reams of data and beam it back to Earth. But not all the information *Curiosity* sends back is of purely scientific interest. When the rover reached its one-year anniversary on the Red Planet, it marked the milestone with a selfie for Facebook. To celebrate the solving of a technical glitch, it tweeted out a close-up photo of its newly fixed drill. And since its launch, *Curiosity* has shared thousands of other photos, updates, and videos with its more than 3 million Twitter followers and 1 million Facebook friends. In other words, in one respect the robotic Martian is just like a rapidly growing number of humans back on twenty-first-century Earth. It's thoroughly plugged into today's defining telecommunications trend: social media.

The Social Media Revolution

Social media sites are internet-based platforms that allow users to create social networks or online communities where they connect and communicate with other people. Different sites vary widely in terms of

Internet users talk with friends, post photos, and do a variety of other things using social media. The number of users on these services has skyrocketed in the early twenty-first century.

their scope, purpose, and functionality, but all social media platforms have certain common elements. They feature content generated by the users themselves. They allow users to interact with content posted by others. And becoming a member typically involves creating a personal profile, an online identity filled with personal information.

The growth of social media worldwide has been explosive. Just 5 percent of Americans used social media platforms in 2005. That number jumped to 50 percent by 2011 and almost 70 percent by 2018. Among Americans aged 18 to 29, social media use is even more common. A whopping 88 percent of Americans in that age bracket are active on social media, according to the Pew Research Center.

In total, more than 3 billion people worldwide now use social media on a regular basis. That comes to more than 40 percent of the world's population. The numbers continue to rise across the globe. In the single year between 2017 and 2018, social media sites gained almost 1 million new users every day from around the world, adding up to a 13 percent increase in social media use worldwide in one year. In some countries, social media use is growing especially fast.

Tools for Change

In June 2010, Egyptian computer engineer Wael Ghonim was browsing Facebook when he saw a photo of a young man named Khaled Said, who had been tortured to death by police in Alexandria, Egypt. The photo haunted Ghonim, bringing home the harsh realities of life under his country's authoritarian government. He created an anonymous Facebook page called "We Are All Khaled Said." Within three days, the page had more than 100,000 followers. Eventually, it even helped to spark a social movement for change, igniting a revolution in early 2011 that toppled Egyptian president Hosni Mubarak.

Similar anti-authoritarian protests broke out in other Middle Eastern countries, including Tunisia, Libya, Bahrain, and Yemen. These were part of a movement known as the Arab Spring—a wave of pro-democracy uprisings that rippled across the Arab world from late 2010 to the end of 2011. Many commentators argue that smartphones and social media were a driving factor in these social revolutions. These powerful digital tools helped people connect with each other, build momentum around a cause, organize collective actions, and share information. They allowed citizen journalists to document events that otherwise would have fallen under the radar and instead propel them into the spotlight.

For example, while only 51 percent of South Korean adults were on social media in 2015, that share rose to 69 percent by 2017.

The rise of social media has fueled a dramatic shift in how we communicate and connect with others. In the early days of the internet, online browsing was primarily a passive pastime—what World Wide Web inventor Tim Berners-Lee called a "read-only" experience.[22] Internet users went online to search for information and to consume it. Websites offered few opportunities for users to collaborate and communicate with each other or to share their own perspectives, ideas, and information. Today, the online experience is fundamentally different. In contrast to the largely static web pages of the 1990s, social media sites have brought a new level of interaction and interconnectedness to the web, making it possible for internet users to engage with people and information from all over the globe—and beyond. As one of *Curiosity*'s fans put it in a comment on the Mars rover's official Facebook page, "To think we can sit in our homes and look at photos taken on Mars a few hours ago is truly amazing."[23]

The Facebook Phenomenon

As the popularity of social media has skyrocketed, so has the number of sites out there. Today, there are hundreds of social media platforms on the web offering different types of online interaction, from social networking to blogging to gaming. Some sites feature a variety of content formats. Twitter, for example, is a popular microblogging platform that allows users to

> **"To think we can sit in our homes and look at photos taken on Mars a few hours ago is truly amazing."[23]**
>
> *– A Facebook follower of the Curiosity rover*

create and share short messages, called tweets, that can consist of anything from text and links to images, videos, and sound clips. Other sites focus on a specific type of media, such as the photo-sharing site Flickr or the video-sharing site YouTube. YouTube, launched in 2005, is now the world's second-most-visited website after Google.

Many social media sites are designed to appeal to any segment of the general public. Others tap into a designated niche and are organized around a specific interest or purpose. For example, people looking to enhance their career opportunities can join professional social networking sites such as LinkedIn. Cyclists and runners can track their workouts and communicate with other sports enthusiasts on fitness sites like Strava, founded in 2009. And book lovers can write and read book reviews, build a virtual bookshelf, and connect with other readers on book recommendation sites like Goodreads, which boasts 80 million members.

But although social media options abound, one site in particular is widely seen as the driving force that shaped the web as we know it today—Facebook, the technological powerhouse that propelled social media into the mainstream. Facebook is a social networking platform that allows members to interact with other users, called friends, by sharing status updates, links, and messages. Users can also create and join interest groups, upload videos, photos, and news articles, and react to the content shared by friends. Facebook wasn't the first social media site out there, but it was the first to achieve widespread popularity. In the process, it created a new paradigm for the online experience.

Founded in 2004 by nineteen-year-old Mark Zuckerberg and fellow Harvard University students, Facebook was originally launched as a social networking site exclusively for Harvard, but it quickly spread to colleges and universities across the country. In 2006,

Facebook's headquarters is in Menlo Park, California. The entrance features a sign with Facebook's iconic thumbs-up "like" icon.

the site was opened to the public, allowing anyone above the age of thirteen to join. "It was built to accomplish a social mission—to make the world more open and connected," Zuckerberg said of his company in a 2012 statement. "At Facebook, we build tools to help people connect with the people they want and share what they want, and by doing this we are extending people's capacity to build and maintain relationships."[24]

Facebook's success was phenomenal, quickly turning CEO Zuckerberg into the world's youngest billionaire. "It turned out that Mark Zuckerberg was right," says internet entrepreneur and tech guru Brian McCullough. "Connecting everyone together—almost the original premise of the web itself—was an incredibly useful and valuable thing."[25] The company's exponential growth bore that out.

Practically overnight, the number of Facebook users skyrocketed. In 2006, the site had 8 million users. In just one year, membership ballooned to 50 million active users. By 2009, the social media empire could claim 350 million users from 180 countries. And in mid-2017, more than half of the world's 4 billion internet users were active on Facebook, about 85 percent of them from outside North America. In the United States, some 68 percent of all adults are now Facebook users. Roughly three-quarters of them visit the site daily. And among Americans aged eighteen to twenty-four, the proportion of Facebook users climbs to 80 percent.

With more than 2 billion active users worldwide, the tech giant has achieved unprecedented global reach and influence. "It has become an overarching common cultural experience for people worldwide, especially young people," David Kirkpatrick writes in his book *The Facebook Effect*. "It may in fact be the fastest growing company of any type in history."[26] In turn, Facebook's success has profoundly influenced the web itself. "Either directly or indirectly, it's the inspiration for just about every social-media feature that has come along since," says technology journalist Farhad Manjoo of Facebook's Newsfeed feature.[27]

> **"It has become an overarching common cultural experience for people worldwide, especially young people. . . . It may in fact be the fastest growing company of any type in history."[26]**
>
> *– David Kirkpatrick, author of* The Facebook Effect, *on the social networking site Facebook*

From Dial-up to Broadband

The social networking revolution unleashed by Facebook has radically changed how we use the internet, including what we do online and how much time we spend doing it. In 2018, the average internet user spent two hours and twenty-two minutes a day on social media sites. That accounts for a full 30 percent of the average internet user's online time—up from 22 percent in 2010. Young people spend even more time engaging with social media. According to a Global Web Index report, online users aged sixteen to twenty-four were plugged into social media for an average of three hours a day in 2018.

All that activity generates an enormous amount of digital data. Every day, more than 4 billion pieces of content are shared on Facebook. That includes 55 million status updates, 150 million comments, and 350 million new photos. More than 100 million photos and videos are uploaded to the media-sharing site Instagram every day. An average of 6,000 tweets are posted on Twitter every second. Four hundred hours of YouTube videos are uploaded every minute, and a staggering 1 billion hours of YouTube videos are watched every day.

Two key advances in telecommunications technology have helped to fuel this explosion of online activity. The first is the growing availability of high-speed internet connections. In the early days of the internet, most people had to make do with dial-up connections by modem, a device that connects to the internet over a phone line. The slow speed of dial-up connections constrained what users could do online. Starting in the early 2000s, however, high-speed broadband connections became increasingly available. These fast internet connections made it possible to browse the web at speeds thirty times faster than sluggish modems would allow.

In 2003 alone, the percentage of Americans with broadband internet service nearly doubled, going from 15 to 25 percent. And by 2018, approximately two-thirds of American adults had broadband internet connections in their homes. High-speed internet connections are now widespread throughout the rest of the developed world too. As a result, for more and more of the world's internet users, it has become increasingly easy to get online, upload and download data, and stream music and video files.

The second crucial piece of infrastructure powering the social media revolution is the rise of mobile computing. "In the technology world, the ultimate success of a new idea is very much dependent on timing," McCullough says.[28] In the case of social media, the timing couldn't have been better. Social media started gaining traction just as another transformative technology was having its breakthrough moment: the smartphone, the perfect tool for social networking.

The Internet in Your Pocket

Smartphones are mobile phones that can connect to the internet and perform many of the functions of a computer. Handheld devices with an internet connection went on the market in the 1990s. For the most part, however, these early devices were slow and clunky, with limited capabilities. Then Apple released the first iPhone in 2007. It was the first mobile computing device to deliver such a high level of functionality and wide range of features in a sleek, user-friendly form. "Every once in a while, a revolutionary product comes along that changes everything," then CEO Steve Jobs exclaimed at the iPhone's announcement event.[29] As it turns out, this boast was no exaggeration.

Apple was a pioneer in the smartphone industry. Its devices remain popular today.

Apple's iPhone sparked a new wave of smartphone technology that continues to evolve. Smartphones are produced by many companies now, and they are rapidly getting faster and more sophisticated. And as smartphones become more affordable, more and more people are buying them. Three percent of Americans owned a smartphone in 2007. A decade later, 80 percent did. Globally, more than two-thirds of people worldwide owned mobile phones as of 2018, and more than half of those devices are smartphones. In fact, for a majority of internet users around the world, mobile devices rather than desktop computers are now the primary way to get online.

The rise of mobile computing has had an enormous impact on telecommunications. Smartphone users now have the ability to get online anywhere and anytime. All the information on the web—and an increasingly connected global social network—is at their fingertips. That constant connectivity makes smartphones the perfect social media gadget, always on hand for sending and receiving messages, posting updates, taking and uploading photos and videos, video chatting, and more.

Experts see a two-way dynamic at work. The popularity of social media creates a bigger market for smartphones. In turn, the availability of smartphones drives up social media use even more. Not surprisingly, this dynamic is having an effect on people's habits. "My smartphone has had a monumental impact on my life," says DeWayne Hamby, a communications specialist from Tennessee. "I used to talk on the phone much more as a social connection, and now I use texts and social media to keep up with everyone."[30] Hamby is far from alone. According to surveys, a majority of Americans under the age of fifty now favor texting over talking on the phone. For teens in particular, that is especially true.

Too Much of a Good Thing?

Together, smartphones and social media are changing people's lives in countless ways, big and small. Social networking makes it possible to connect with people from all over the world, breaking down barriers and facilitating the sharing of ideas and information. However, critics worry that mobile devices and social media may be creating a culture of addiction, fueling an obsessive need to remain connected. "Social media has been described as more addictive than cigarettes and alcohol," says Shirley Cramer, chief executive of the Royal Society for Public Health in the United Kingdom.[31] Smartphones compound the effect. "Mobile technology means we're always on, always plugged in, always stimulated, always in a constant state of self-presentation," MIT professor Sherry Turkle says.[32]

> **"Mobile technology means we're always on, always plugged in, always stimulated, always in a constant state of self-presentation."[32]**
>
> – MIT professor Sherry Turkle

Three-quarters of smartphone users check their phone and social media apps for updates as soon as they wake up in the morning. More than half say they even check their phones during the night. That pattern of dependence continues throughout the day for many smartphone users. Michael Saylor, founder of the software company MicroStrategy and author of *The Mobile Wave*, says he checks his phone at least once a minute. "I must look at it 500 times a day, or 1,000 times a day," the business executive says.[33]

Overall, more than 31 percent of Americans who connect to the internet via mobile device say they are almost constantly connected throughout the day. For adults aged eighteen to twenty-nine, that number jumps to 39 percent. By comparison, among internet users who do not connect via smartphone or other mobile device, just 5 percent say they go online almost constantly. One 2016 study estimated that, on average, American smartphone users tap, type, swipe, or click on their mobile devices more than 2,600 times a day.

All this screen time comes at a price, critics warn. Although mobile phones and social networking make it easier than ever to connect with people around the globe, at the same time they are eroding face-to-face relationships with people in our daily lives, according to a number of researchers. Studies also show that heavy smartphone users have a harder time performing certain cognitive tasks, such as staying focused. And social media and smartphone use may even take a toll on mental health and well-being.

It's hard to prove that this link is causal or to identify exactly what underpins it, but many researchers think that social media can trigger feelings of inadequacy and low self-esteem. This is because social networking exposes people to a steady stream of perfectly edited pictures and interesting status updates that can leave them feeling that their own lives don't measure up. This reaction is so common that a term has been coined for it: FOMO, meaning "fear of missing out." It was officially added to the *Oxford English Dictionary* in 2013.

This explanation resonates with Shannon McLaughlin, an eighteen-year-old from Blackburn, England. She pins much of the blame on social media for her own struggles with anxiety and depression. Scrolling through Facebook and Instagram made her feel bad about herself. "Seeing that everyone was happy and enjoying life made me feel so much worse," she says. "In fact, it made me feel like I was doing something wrong."[34]

The solution, experts say, is not to turn our backs on the high-tech world of mobile devices and social networking. That is both impossible and unnecessary. These digital tools are now firmly part of twenty-first-century reality. They offer tremendous potential that can be harnessed for good. Used right, they broaden our horizons and put a wealth of knowledge in our hands. The key is to maintain the right balance. McLaughlin found that balance by taking more time to make off-screen friends. She also started volunteering regularly. Connecting face-to-face with real people has made a huge difference in her

The Downside of Social Media

Social media and smartphones have been hailed as tools for freedom and democracy, but recently critics have begun to worry that there is a dark side to these digital technologies. Social media sites can easily turn into echo chambers—online bubbles where people mostly hear perspectives that echo what they already believe. This can deepen political divisions and fuel social unrest. As journalist Nicholas Carr says, "It clearly adds to the polarization of society and people getting more and more extreme in their views."

All too often social media platforms degenerate into toxic environments where hate speech abounds. And these sites have proven themselves to be perfect vehicles for spreading misinformation and fake news. Worries about the disruptive effects of social media came to the mainstream after the 2016 US presidential election. Throughout the campaign, fake news spread like wildfire on sites like Facebook and Twitter. In many cases, fake stories were shared more times on social media sites than factual news stories.

Quoted in Lynne Peeples, "Can't Put Down the Phone? How Smartphones Are Changing Our Brains—and Lives," NBC News, December 14, 2018. www.nbcnews.com.

life, the teen says. "It's so important for young people to make real connections without hiding behind a text message or a happy social media post," she emphasizes. "I think it's important for young people to look up from their phones and focus more on the world around them, and the amazing connections that they can make there."[35]

Chapter 3

How Have Digital Devices Changed Daily Life?

S martphones are miniature computers capable of tapping into a globally connected web from anywhere. But these days it's not just phones and computers that connect to the internet. More and more of the objects in our daily life—from household appliances to light bulbs to entertainment systems—are designed to interface with the web, collecting and sharing data just the way our smartphones do. These internet-enabled gadgets are known as smart devices or smart technology. Processing power and wireless networking technology transform everyday objects into futuristic devices with a wide range of functions.

For example, smart televisions connect wirelessly to the web, enabling viewers to stream content from online video services such as Netflix, Hulu, or YouTube. Smart watches can send and receive texts and emails or monitor a person's fitness levels, syncing with an app to track health statistics over time. Smart beds monitor a user's sleep patterns and can automatically adjust the firmness or temperature of the mattress. And smart washers and dryers can be controlled remotely by smartphone so that a person can start a load of laundry when he is away and find it waiting for him when

A wide variety of smart appliances and devices can now be controlled remotely. Advancing computer and networking technologies have made this revolution possible.

he walks in the door. There are even smart toilets, smart pet food dispensers, smart speakers, and smart garments—fabrics with digital components stitched in that can perform a range of functions, such as automatically heating up or cooling down.

The Internet of Things

Just about anything that can be embedded with electronic circuitry and connected wirelessly to the internet can be turned "smart." And as the market for smart gadgets grows, that's what's happening to more and more everyday devices. In 2017, more than 8 billion devices worldwide were connected to the internet, surpassing the total number of people in the world. By 2018, the number of connected devices in use worldwide reached more than 17 billion.

The total collection of all these smart devices can be thought of as an interconnected system—a networked world of connected devices. This is known as the Internet of Things (IoT). The IoT enables devices to exchange data with other devices via the internet, creating a rapidly growing web of things that are all communicating with each other. This emerging technology has enormous potential to radically change how we live and work, redefining how we relate to the things around us. "The Internet of Things will touch almost every part of our lives in the years ahead," says tech writer Samuel Greengard. It "promises to alter our lives faster and more profoundly than any technology in history."[36] One sphere of life where IoT technology is already making significant inroads is the household, where more and more of the home appliances we rely on are being reconfigured with smart technology to rewire how we go about our daily routines.

Smart Homes

The first commercially available smart appliance came to the market in the United States in 2009. It was a hot water heater produced by the multinational corporation General Electric. The appliance could link up with a home's utility meter, measuring electricity use. It also allowed users to switch to an electricity-saving mode when appropriate. Since then, the number of connected household devices has skyrocketed. So has the demand. "People just can't get enough of smart devices," says tech journalist Dylan Martin, noting that there was a 66 percent uptick in the number of consumers planning to buy smart home

Smart security systems allow people to view the status of their home through cameras and sensors. Homeowners can check on their home no matter where they are, as long as they have an internet connection.

devices in 2018 as compared to the previous year.[37] Overall, global sales for smart home devices reached $53 billion in 2018, according to the market research firm Strategy Analytics.

Consumers can now buy smart versions of a huge range of household items, from kitchenware like slow cookers, coffee makers, toasters, and microwaves to items like mirrors, light fixtures, and window shades. There are smart doorbells that send an alert when someone is at the door and smart locks that can be checked remotely by cell phone—a boon for forgetful people prone to worrying about whether they remembered to lock up on their way out.

Smart security cameras sync with a mobile phone to allow homeowners to monitor their homes for suspicious activity even when they are miles away. And the built-in freshness trackers and cameras on smart refrigerators can keep track of expiration dates on perishables. The owner can check their fridge by smartphone to see if they need to visit the supermarket on the way home. Some types of smart refrigerators can even sync with a shopping app to add and order items automatically from a virtual grocery list.

Any of the various smart home appliances on the market today can be set up and run separately. But when several different smart devices are connected together into a networked system, then the whole home turns smart. These various devices can be coordinated through a central hub, a single app or piece of software used to control them. Because they are wirelessly connected, the devices can share data to set off a chain of automated functions.

As an example of connected devices sharing data with each other, consider the Luna smart mattress, which can be added to any bed. Sensors track a person's sleep cycles, monitoring body temperature, heart rate, breathing patterns, and other relevant data. If there are other connected smart devices in the home, Luna can share the data it collects with those devices to trigger a set of programmed responses. For instance, when Luna's sensors detect that the user is entering the light phase of sleep that precedes waking up, the system can tell the home's smart coffee maker to start making the morning brew. It can also activate the mechanized window shades, instruct the networked thermostat to turn up the heat, turn on the morning news on the smart TV, start preheating the smart oven for the breakfast muffins to bake, and set in motion any number of other processes.

Getting Smarter about the Environment

Many consumers are attracted to smart devices because of their convenience. For interior decorator Iantha Carley, for example, the ability to switch on her lights and appliances from anywhere is a big selling point. "That's really helpful," she says. "I think it's great to be

Privacy and Security Risks

Smart devices are more popular than ever, but there are downsides to the increased connectivity that comes with the Internet of Things. Each connected device collects an ongoing stream of data about its users and their habits. Yet the companies that produce these devices are often not transparent about how they collect, store, and use all that information—or about what they do to protect it. "The selling point for these well-connected objects is added convenience and better safety," says Zeynep Tufekci, a sociologist at the University of North Carolina who studies the effects of the internet on society. "In reality, it is a fast-motion train wreck in privacy and security."

Once a person's data has been collected, where it ends up is out of their control. It could be sold to other companies. Theoretically, government agencies could even tap into it for surveillance purposes. And the data could end up in the hands of hackers with criminal intent if the companies collecting it suffer a data breach. According to a 2018 report by finance and technology news site *Business Insider*, cybersecurity attacks on companies are on the rise.

Zeynep Tufekci, "Why 'Smart' Objects May Be a Dumb Idea," New York Times, August 10, 2015. www.nytimes.com.

able to control your lights, your HVAC, turn on your fireplace on a cold winter's day right before you get home."[38] But some smart appliances can also align with a loftier goal—reducing energy consumption and helping the environment. "As climate change becomes a fact of life and fossil fuel reduction becomes critically important, efficient energy management in the home will play a major factor in sustainability goals," says Kent Dickson, CEO of the IoT company Yonomi. "The smart home represents a bright spot in this transition to a cleaner future."[39]

The ability to control smart lights remotely via cell phone means that someone who forgets to turn off the lights before leaving the house can use her phone to flip the switch from afar. Smart lights can also sync with software that analyzes how much electricity is used across the house to help consumers identify wasteful patterns. Similarly, other appliances like washers, dryers, and dishwashers can be integrated with energy-management apps that help them run more efficiently. And smart thermostats not only can be operated remotely but also can be programmed to automatically shut off the heating and cooling system when it is not needed or to run it at a more energy-efficient time of day.

Eventually, these smart devices in individual homes will be able to link up to a city-wide "smart grid." This is the term used to refer to a

> "As climate change becomes a fact of life and fossil fuel reduction becomes critically important, efficient energy management in the home will play a major factor in sustainability goals. The smart home represents a bright spot in this transition to a cleaner future."[39]
>
> – Kent Dickson, CEO of the IoT company Yonomi

modernized version of the electric grid, the network of transmission lines that deliver electricity from the power plant to an area's homes and businesses. The revamped smart grid of the future will have sensors and smart meters to measure energy usage along the transmission lines. These meters will connect to a cellular wireless network that enables two-way communication with the utility meters in homes and businesses. This will make it easier for the utility company to reduce waste and optimize energy usage. The utility company will also be able to quickly address power outages and route power where it's needed most at a given time.

Ultimately, urban planners envision the smart grid as just one component of an entire "smart city"—a city or other geographic area where all the public infrastructure is integrated with smart technology to share data and run seamlessly. For example, the smart city might include streetlights that automatically adapt to the time of day or to weather conditions like fog. Roadside sensors could collect data on traffic congestion, and parking meters could collect data on whether spaces are full or empty, producing a grid of data updated in real time. All this data could be fed into an app. With a tap on their smartphones, drivers in the smart city would be able to avoid traffic congestion or easily find a parking space. Similar smart technology could be used to guide the most efficient use of public resources in everything from how road maintenance crews are dispatched to how waste is managed.

Machine Intelligence

The Internet of Things depends on many feats of engineering, including advances in computer processing, electronics, wireless internet technology, high-tech sensors, and data storage. But the heart of smart technology is artificial intelligence (AI). This field of computer science aims to create machines and computers that can approximate human functions like problem-solving, language recognition, and visual processing—the ability to recognize and categorize images.

Advances in machine learning are driving a boom in AI research. Machine learning uses complex computational algorithms to create systems that can process large amounts of data, recognize patterns in the data, and improve their performance on a given task over time. Algorithms are sets of instructions or codes that tell a computer how to complete a task. The algorithms used in machine learning enable a machine or computer to figure out how to do a task rather than having to be pre-programmed with a set of explicit rules. In essence, these algorithms make it possible for the system to learn from new data as it goes along. Thus, the more data a machine-learning system is fed, the better it gets at a task.

> **"In the twentieth century, computers were brains without senses—they only knew what we told them. In the twenty-first century, because of the Internet of Things, computers can sense things for themselves."[40]**
>
> *– Kevin Ashton, British tech entrepreneur*

Machine-learning algorithms make today's devices vastly more capable and flexible than in the past, when computers were limited by what programmers had coded them to do. That was a significant limitation because the amount of data that a human programmer can manually input into a machine pales in comparison to the amount of possibly relevant data out in the world. "In the twentieth century, computers were brains without senses—they only knew what we told them," explains Kevin Ashton, the British tech entrepreneur who coined the phrase *Internet of Things*. "In the twenty-first century, because of the Internet of Things, computers can sense things for themselves."[40]

Artificial intelligence and machine learning power many of the smart devices that are a part of everyday life. Voice-activated digital assistants like Apple's Siri and Amazon's Alexa use machine-learning algorithms to get better at understanding questions and commands and tailoring responses to fit the particular user. And thermostats made by American manufacturer Nest Labs don't just turn on or off according to a pre-programmed set of functions. Instead, they adjust how they function over time by picking up on the habits and patterns of the people living in the house. For example, if the owners consistently turn the heat down when they leave for work and bump it up again when they return, the Nest thermostat will learn to automatically make those adjustments on its own.

Robots at Work—and at the Wheel

Thanks to AI-based technologies, advances in robotics are also changing how we live and how we work. In the household, robots like the Roomba vacuum are taking over daily chores. The self-navigating vacuum uses sensors, cameras, and computer algorithms to map out and learn the spaces in a room. Designed by iRobot, the popular robotic cleaner is able to detect dirt with its sensors, skillfully weave around obstacles, and automatically change its settings to deal with different floor surfaces.

In the workplace, more and more tasks are being automated, or performed by machines without direct human control. For example, if you order a Roomba from Amazon, chances are a robot will help to get it from the warehouse to your doorstep. Amazon began using robots in its fulfillment centers in 2013. In 2018, the giant corporation had more than 100,000 robots in warehouses worldwide. Fleets of orange robots scuttle from shelf to shelf, sorting and carting items. Optical sensors guide them through the giant facilities, where they use computer vision technology to navigate around obstacles and to recognize and categorize items ready to be packed. Able to carry up to 1,500 pounds (680 kg) at a time, the AI-powered robots can do in 15 minutes what it previously took human workers more than an hour to finish.

Robots are not new. The first programmable robots date back to the 1960s. But what is new is the complexity of the tasks that robots are now capable of tackling. As AI becomes more advanced, robots and other computer-controlled systems are becoming increasingly sophisticated, capable of taking over more and more human functions. These technological innovations are fueling one of the fastest growing areas in robotics—the development of robot cars, also called self-driving, driverless, or autonomous vehicles.

Self-driving vehicles are cars and trucks that can drive fully independently, without human drivers needing to take control. High-tech sensors enable self-driving vehicles to construct a map of their surroundings. Software analyzes the inputs from those sensors to tell the vehicle's controls how to steer, accelerate, navigate, and brake. Complex algorithms and statistical modeling help the vehicle obey traffic rules, navigate around obstacles, respond to road conditions, and distinguish objects around it.

The experimental technology still has a long way to go, but many manufacturers are racing to get their own prototypes on the road. Google started developing self-driving systems in 2009. By 2016, the tech giant had almost 60 test vehicles on the road in four

Today's self-driving cars look similar to their traditional car counterparts. However, they can usually be distinguished by the array of sensors mounted on the roof and body.

states, logging 2 million miles (3.2 million km) in test drives. Nissan, BMW, Tesla, and many other major automakers have also launched self-driving vehicle programs, as has the ride-sharing pioneer Uber.

In October 2016, the Uber-funded start-up Otto became the first company to make a commercial delivery with a self-driving vehicle. Their driverless 18-wheeler drove roughly 120 miles (190 km) from Fort Collins, Colorado, to Colorado Springs. The big rig was delivering 2,000 cases of beer. And in December 2018, Google spinoff Waymo logged another important milestone for self-driving vehicles. The company launched the world's first commercial self-driving taxi service. Riders in a suburb of Phoenix, Arizona, can use a smartphone app to hail a self-driving minivan. While the company tests out the system, it will keep backup human drivers behind the wheel for safety. But experts say the milestone represents a significant turning point for driverless technology.

Winners and Losers

Surveys show that many Americans have doubts about driverless technology. According to a 2017 Pew Research Center poll, 54 percent of Americans are either somewhat or very worried about the development of self-driving vehicles. In a 2018 survey by HNTB Corporation, an infrastructure solutions firm, 55 percent said they wouldn't ride in an autonomous vehicle. At the same time, 70 percent said they expected self-driving vehicles to be common within the next fifteen years.

Public skepticism about self-driving vehicles is largely driven by fears that the cars are not safe. Recently, these fears have been fueled by a number of headline-grabbing accidents. For example, a self-driving test car developed by Uber struck and killed a pedestrian in Tempe, Arizona, in March 2018. In response, Uber pulled its self-driving test cars from the road. Experts say, however, that when the technology is perfected, self-driving cars have the potential to be much safer than human-controlled ones. Vehicle crashes are currently the second leading cause of accidental deaths in the United States. According to the National Highway Traffic Safety Administration, auto accidents claim an average of 110 lives a day in the United States. Worldwide, car crashes are responsible for approximately 1.3 million

Self-driving vehicles must be aware of their surroundings in all directions at all times. They track pedestrians, other vehicles, and any road hazards that might appear.

deaths a year. In the case of 94 percent of serious crashes, human error is to blame.

Removing humans from the wheel will eliminate the causes of error, proponents of self-driving cars say. "As self-driving technology continues to advance, these vehicles will ultimately prove to be safer, especially when compared to the nearly 40,000 US traffic fatalities that occur each year from people-driven vehicles," says HNTB's Jim Barbaresso, pointing out that driverless cars won't succumb to tiredness, absentmindedness, or road rage. "Technology refinements onboard the vehicles as well as in the infrastructure along our roadways will eventually enable us to drive traffic fatalities to near zero."[41]

In addition to saving lives, self-driving vehicles could make a difference in other ways. For example, being able to hitch a ride without taking the wheel would help those who are unable to drive themselves, such as some people with disabilities or elderly people. "These people would gain mobility," says Carnegie Mellon professor Raj Rajkumar. "It would greatly help the 1.5 million legally blind Americans and the more than 5 million disabled people who can't drive."[42] But the overall costs to society could also be great. Experts predict that self-driving vehicles could threaten the livelihood of many people, including truckers and taxi drivers. In total, as many as 5 million jobs could be lost in just the United States.

Continued advances in artificial intelligence, robotics, the Internet of Things, and smart technology are set to transform life in many ways. Some of these transformations may make life easier, safer, and better. For example, they may give us new tools for tackling serious problems, such as climate change. But the technologies of the future could also create new problems and challenges, such as greater unemployment and wider inequality. Society's growing dependence on digital technologies could deepen the digital divide, the gap between those who have access to computer technology and those who do not.

Many people see reasons to be optimistic. Ray Kurzweil, director of engineering at Google, thinks that the benefits of artificial technology outweigh the potential risks. "My view is not that AI is going to displace us," the American inventor says. "It's going to enhance us. It does already."[43] Similarly, in a Pew Research Center survey of experts, a majority predicted that IoT technology will have largely beneficial effects.

"My view is not that AI is going to displace us. It's going to enhance us. It does already."[43]

– Ray Kurzweil, director of engineering at Google

Both the optimists and the pessimists agree on one thing, though—for good or for ill, the effects of these new technologies will be far-reaching and widespread, affecting just about everyone and everything. Profound transformations are already taking place in many areas. Some of the most dramatic are in the field of medicine, where innovations in robotics, artificial intelligence, and smart technology are transforming health care.

Chapter 4

How Are Medical Advances Improving Lives?

Shimmering in sequins, Adrianne Haslet-Davis glides across the stage with her dance partner at the Vancouver Conference Center in Canada in March 2014. With nimble footwork and impeccable rhythm, she executes flawless twirls and dips in sync to music by Spanish pop legend Enrique Iglesias. As a professional ballroom dancer, the thirty-three-year-old Bostonian is no stranger to the stage.

This time, however, is different. In 2013, Haslet-Davis had been a spectator at the Boston Marathon when terrorists set off a pair of bombs in the crowd. Her lower left leg was ripped apart by shrapnel, and doctors had to amputate it. Now, just one year later, Haslet-Davis is performing in public again for the first time since the traumatic event—a feat made possible by recent advances in robotics and engineering that are revolutionizing how prostheses work.

Haslet-Davis's movements look effortless and natural, but each step of her left leg is powered by the whir of machinery hidden inside the sleek synthetic sheath of a prosthesis, or artificial limb. A complex web of sensors and circuits controls an artificial calf muscle, activated by a small motor that channels energy into a spring. Tiny computer chips run complicated algorithms to track and adjust every element

One year after the marathon bombing, Haslet-Davis returned to the Boston Marathon. She was assisted by her brothers and by a high-tech prosthetic leg.

of motion, down to the speed, angle, and force of the heel strike. The result is an unprecedented range and fluidity of motion—a robotic leg that feels and acts like the real thing.

This engineering marvel is the brainchild of MIT researcher Hugh Herr, who is also an amputee. In 1982, when he was just seventeen, the Pennsylvania native lost both legs to frostbite after a failed mountaineering expedition. Today, Herr heads the biomechatronics group at the MIT Media Lab, a research team that integrates biology, mechanics, and electronics to create pioneering devices like the BiOM Ankle System. That's the prototype for Haslet-Davis's custom-made prosthesis. Clinical trials in 2011 showed it to be the first artificial leg able to simulate the way natural limbs function. "Every person should have the right to live their life without disability if they so choose," Herr says.[44]

Bionic Limbs

In the United States alone, roughly 2 million people have had a limb surgically removed because of injury or illness. Around the world, more than 1 million new amputations are performed every year. Millions of other people across the globe are living with impaired mobility not because of amputation but because of paralysis. But thanks to research by Herr and other scientists and engineers, many people with physical disabilities are having their lives transformed by a new generation of bionic limbs capable of restoring greater functionality than ever before.

One of these people is Doug McIntosh from Westhill, Scotland. After losing his right hand and forearm to cancer in 1997, the father of three used a split-hook prosthesis for twenty years. The device could open, close, and rotate, but it didn't allow any more complex movements. In 2017, the fifty-six-year-old became one of the first to test out an experimental bionic hand developed by researchers at Newcastle University in the United Kingdom. Outfitted with an AI-enhanced computer vision system, the device uses machine-learning algorithms to recognize objects and determine the correct grip needed to pick them up successfully. A camera takes rapid-fire pictures of the object in front of it, feeding the data to a software control system that triggers the appropriate hand motions

3D Printing in Medicine

Implants

In 2012, doctors were able to save the life of an infant whose bronchial tube had collapsed by implanting a 3D-printed synthetic windpipe. And in 2013, researchers created the first 3D-printed outer ear that resembles and works like the real thing. Since then, scientists have also been able to 3D-print ears using a patient's own stem cells—cells that can turn into any type of cell in the body.

Blood Vessels

Scientists are developing techniques for creating 3D-printed blood vessels from stem cells—an important first step toward being able to create artificial organs. 3D-printed blood vessels will also be able to help patients whose blood vessels are damaged or clogged because of cardiovascular disease.

Organs

Scientists have not yet been able to create 3D-printed organs that really function and can viably be transplanted into human patients, but they are making great strides in that direction. Researchers have successfully 3D-printed organ tissues—including kidney, liver, and even heart tissue—using human cells as "bio-ink."

Surgical Applications

Using 3D printing, surgeons are able to create patient-specific models or templates of a surgery site. These 3D guides help surgeons plan out and perform complex procedures, including jaw surgery, knee replacement operations, neurosurgical procedures, and facial reconstructions. They are also a valuable training resource for medical students.

Researchers are now using 3D printing as a cost-effective way to help patients. 3D printing is a process of creating a 3D physical object from a computer-generated digital model. Typically, this involves laying down many thin layers of a material in succession.

within milliseconds—ten times faster than any other currently available prosthetic hand.

"The beauty of this system is that it's much more flexible and the hand is able to pick up novel objects—which is crucial since in everyday life people effortlessly pick up a variety of objects that they have never seen before," says Dr. Kianoush Nazarpour, one of the team's lead researchers.[45] McIntosh describes the innovation as a "huge leap forward." "To have the option of a hand that not only looks realistic but also works like a real hand would be an amazing breakthrough and transform the recovery time—both physically and mentally—for many amputees," he says.[46]

Mind Control

Advanced computer technologies are rapidly improving the design and function of prosthetic devices. Some researchers are even experimenting with methods of linking computerized functions directly to the brain to create prostheses controlled by the power of thought. Such technologies, called brain-computer interfaces, work by tapping into neural activity in areas of the brain that control motion. This brain activity continues even when a person loses the ability to move a limb because of amputation or paralysis. Scientists implant electrodes in the brain to record the activity of individual neurons. Computational algorithms then decode those neural patterns and translate them into signals sent to sensors that activate the robotic or paralyzed limb.

Researchers from Case Western Reserve University in Ohio conducted a clinical trial of the revolutionary procedure in 2017. Eight years after a bicycle accident deprived him of the ability to move from the neck down, fifty-three-year-old Bill Kochevar became the first paralyzed person to control his own arm through his thoughts.

"It was amazing because I thought about moving my arm, and it did," Kochevar says.[47] Using the system, the Ohio resident was able to grasp a fork and cup to eat and drink unassisted for the first time since his accident. "This is a big step," says Bob Kirsch, professor of biomedical engineering at Case Western Reserve University. "We've shown the feasibility of recording someone's movement intentions and then making their own arm make those movements."[48]

Researchers stress that the procedure is still highly experimental and not ready for use outside of the lab. Technology is advancing so rapidly, however, that experts predict that the bionic devices of the future will connect seamlessly to the brain. People with paralyzed or amputated limbs will be able to recover not just the power of movement but also the ability to feel sensations. "It will be possible to use technology to sculpt the human body in any form that we want," Herr says.[49]

> **"It will be possible to use technology to sculpt the human body in any form that we want."[49]**
>
> – *Hugh Herr, MIT researcher*

The Robot Doctor Is In

The same transformative technologies powering today's smart prostheses are also behind remarkable advances in other areas of medicine. From diagnostic imaging to AI systems that monitor patients' vital signs, technology-driven innovations in health care are changing how medical professionals dispense medicine, diagnose diseases, and even perform surgery in the twenty-first century.

Robot-assisted surgery is now a reality in major hospitals around the world. In 2000, the US Food and Drug Administration (FDA) approved the da Vinci Surgical System—the first machine of its kind,

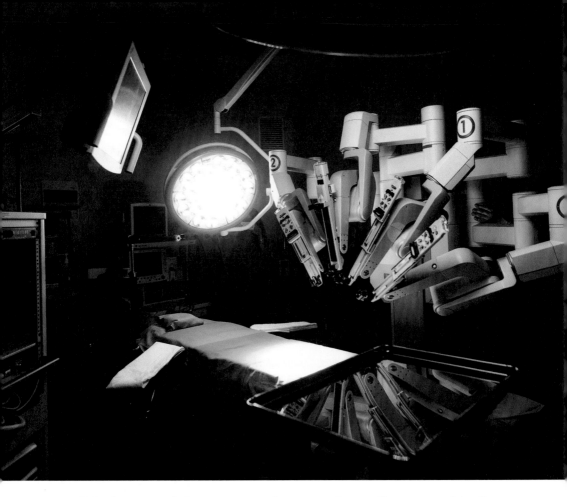

Robotic systems help surgeons perform procedures with more precision than is possible with traditional techniques. Eventually, robots may be able to do surgeries entirely autonomously.

named after Renaissance-era artist and inventor Leonardo da Vinci. In 2015 alone, it was used in more than 650,000 operations worldwide. Equipped with a 3D camera and robotic arms that are controlled remotely by a human surgeon, it is capable of making smaller, more precise incisions than handheld tools can. This means an easier and faster recovery time for patients, plus less risk of infection. "I just bumped into one of my patients being discharged three to four days after an operation using the robot, instead of the three to four weeks it would have taken in the past," Pardeep Kumar, a surgeon at the Royal Marsden Hospital in London, told the *Guardian* newspaper in 2014.[50]

While robots are helping in the operating room, smart technology and artificial intelligence are helping with diagnosis and treatment. Thanks to Stanford University researchers, anyone with a smartphone may soon have access to a free diagnostic tool to screen for melanoma, the most deadly form of skin cancer. In 2017, an interdisciplinary team of computer scientists and dermatologists at the California university joined forces to create an algorithm-driven AI system to detect cancerous skin lesions. The team used deep learning, a type of artificial intelligence modeled after neural networks in the brain, to train the computer system to recognize different skin cancers in digital images. The result is a sophisticated diagnostic tool that can distinguish benign, or harmless, moles from cancerous skin lesions as well as or better than a panel of twenty-one board-certified dermatologists.

"My main eureka moment was when I realized just how ubiquitous smartphones will be," says Andre Esteva, one of the lead researchers. "Everyone will have a supercomputer in their pockets with a number of sensors in it, including a camera. What if we could use it to visually screen for skin cancer? Or other ailments?"[51]

The Genome Project

Innovations in computing power, data analytics, and artificial intelligence are changing how health care is practiced. These high-tech advances have also facilitated what is arguably the

> "Everyone will have a supercomputer in their pockets with a number of sensors in it, including a camera. What if we could use it to visually screen for skin cancer? Or other ailments?"[51]
>
> – Andre Esteva, medical researcher

greatest milestone in medical research in the twenty-first century: the decoding of the human genome, the biological blueprint of the human body.

Completed in 2003, the Human Genome Project was an epic thirteen-year quest to map out the entire set of genes that govern how humans develop and function. Thousands of researchers around the world collaborated on the effort, using a painstaking process called DNA sequencing. This involves determining the sequence, or order, of the chemical building blocks that make up DNA molecules, the basic hereditary material found in every cell. DNA sequencing allows researchers to identify the genes encoded in segments of DNA. It's a process that scientists compare to deciphering an instruction book that spells out our genetic heritage. Cracking that genetic code "represents one of the remarkable achievements in the history of science," MIT biologist Eric Lander says.[52] And to a large degree, that achievement was fueled by new technologies that made it easier to sequence the data.

Today, advances in complex computational algorithms and AI have made DNA sequencing even simpler, faster, and cheaper. Much of the sequencing process is now automated. This has led to a tidal wave of research in genomics, or the study of genomes—and a flood of medical breakthroughs. Building on the success of the Human Genome Project, other large-scale gene sequencing projects around the world, such as the Cancer Genome Atlas in the United States and the 100,000 Genomes Project in the United Kingdom, are collecting a growing pool of data on the genetics of disease.

By comparing the genome sequences of healthy cells with those of diseased cells, scientists are able to identify specific gene mutations that appear to be linked with certain diseases. So far, researchers have been able to identify more than 4,000 different kinds of gene mutations associated with a wide range of health conditions, from aggressive breast cancer to atopic dermatitis, a skin disorder. More than 2,000 genetic tests have been created for different diseases. Such tests do not only help doctors diagnose sick patients. They can also help people evaluate their future risks for various diseases, including Alzheimer's, Parkinson's disease, and macular degeneration, an eye disease. Those who learn that they have a genetic predisposition for a certain disease can then be more proactive about managing their health care and making lifestyle and nutrition changes to increase their odds of staying healthy.

Do-It-Yourself Health

Technology is putting more and more tools in people's hands to help them stay on top of their own health. Computer automation has made DNA testing so cheap and widespread that mail-order tests retail for around one hundred dollars. Consumers can drop a saliva sample in the mail and get back a readout of their genome. These tests offer insight into a person's ancestry as well as information about their risk factors for certain inherited diseases. Experts caution, though, that the accuracy of commercial tests may vary and the results need to be taken with a grain of salt.

Smart health gadgets are also becoming widely available. Wearable gadgets such as fitness trackers help motivate people to stay active while also tracking biometrics such as heart rate, blood pressure, and breathing. These devices connect wirelessly to a smartphone app that helps people monitor their vitals over time. Some personal devices can help detect signs of serious conditions, such as atrial fibrillation, a heart rhythm disorder that is associated with a heightened risk of stroke. The results can be shared wirelessly with health-care practitioners, helping them to monitor their patients outside of the doctor's office.

Ultimately, scientists hope to be able to use genomics to find DNA-based cures that target the genetic roots of diseases. Already, medical researchers have made some remarkable breakthroughs. In November 2018, for example, the FDA approved the first drug designed to treat cancers based on their specific genetic characteristics rather than on where they are located in the body. "This type of drug development program, which enrolled patients with different tumors but a common gene mutation, wouldn't have been possible a decade ago because we knew a lot less about such cancer mutations," FDA Commissioner Dr. Scott Gottlieb says.[53]

> **"This type of drug development program, which enrolled patients with different tumors but a common gene mutation, wouldn't have been possible a decade ago because we knew a lot less about such cancer mutations."[53]**
>
> – *Dr. Scott Gottlieb, FDA Commissioner*

Doctoring Genes

In 2015, Layla Richards, a one-year-old from London, became the first patient ever to receive genetically engineered immune cells from a donor. When she was just three months old, Layla was diagnosed with acute lymphoblastic leukemia, the most common type of childhood cancer. Although the disease is typically highly responsive to treatment, Layla's case was particularly aggressive. Chemotherapy failed to curb the cancer. Immunotherapy—a treatment designed to boost a patient's immune cells so that they can fight off the cancer—was not an option because the little girl was so sick and weak that she hardly had any functioning immune cells left at all.

As a last resort, Layla's desperate parents agreed to try a pioneering procedure never before tested on humans. Doctors took immune cells from a healthy donor and modified them using gene editing. They added a new gene that was specifically designed to target cancer cells, and they disabled a second gene that otherwise would have made Layla's body reject the donor cells as foreign. The engineered donor cells were then transplanted into Layla's body. Within a month, all the cancerous cells in her bone marrow were gone. As of 2018, the little girl was still leukemia-free. "This is the first time human cells, engineered in this particular way, have been given back to a patient and that was a big step for us," says Waseem Qasim, a professor at the University College London and the doctor who developed Layla's treatment. Paul Veys, director of the Bone Marrow Transplant team at the Great Ormond Street Hospital in London, describes the outcome as "almost like a miracle."[54]

The CRISPR Revolution

Although research on gene editing still has a long way to go, scientists hope that the technique can eventually lead to breakthrough treatments for a huge range of diseases. One gene-editing method in particular has propelled the field forward by leaps and bounds—a technique known as CRISPR, short for "clustered regularly interspaced short palindromic repeats." Developed in 2012 by Berkeley biochemist Jennifer Doudna and her French colleague Emmanuelle Charpentier, CRISPR harnesses a naturally occurring process in the immune systems of bacteria to edit genes. The procedure is widely regarded as a game-changer for biomedical research. Simpler, cheaper, more versatile, and more accurate than

Jennifer Doudna's CRISPR technique shows major promise in the field of gene editing. She has spoken about the breakthrough at a variety of genetics conferences.

previous DNA-editing techniques, CRISPR allows scientists to target specific regions of the genome with great precision.

With the ability to delete, replace, or repair any sequence of DNA in the human genome, scientists could potentially cure any disorder caused by an identifiable gene mutation. In a laboratory setting, researchers have already successfully used CRISPR to correct defective genes associated with a slew of serious disorders. Among others, these include sickle cell anemia, a serious blood disorder; Duchenne muscular dystrophy, which causes progressive muscle degeneration; and cystic fibrosis, a life-threatening inherited disease that causes thickened mucus to build up in the lungs and other organs.

In the future, scientists may be able to use gene editing in many other contexts to make an impact on human health. For example, scientists are experimenting with ways of genetically manipulating mosquito DNA to prevent the insects from being able to transmit infectious diseases such as malaria and Zika. Other recent experiments have focused on altering the DNA of pigs to make their organs a better match for human transplants.

Not all of the potential applications of the powerful biotechnology are uncontroversial, however. In November 2018, biophysicist He Jiankui of the Southern University of Science and Technology in Shenzhen, China, announced that he had used CRISPR to alter the DNA of two human embryos, resulting in the birth of the world's first genetically edited babies—twin girls genetically manipulated to be resistant to HIV, the virus that causes AIDS. Scientists around the world reacted with alarm. Many condemned He's work as an irresponsible breach of medical ethics. Marcy Darnovsky, executive director of the Center for Genetics and Society in California, called it "reckless experimentation on human beings."[55] Kathy Niakan, a biologist at the Francis Crick Institute in London, said, "It is impossible to overstate how irresponsible, unethical and dangerous this is at the moment."[56]

He's experiment on human embryos was controversial because it involved editing germ-line cells, reproductive cells containing the genetic code that gets passed down from generation to generation. In effect, germ-line editing introduces permanent changes into the gene pool. This is very different from what happens when conventional gene therapy is used to treat sick patients. In those cases, edits are made to specific cells that do not affect future offspring.

For the time being, the consensus in the scientific community is that genetically altering the human germ-line is too risky and unsafe—at least given the current state of technology. Gene-editing attempts sometimes produce accidental edits to the wrong genes. Even when no mistakes occur, unforeseen consequences may arise. Tweaking one particular gene to produce a desired outcome may trigger unintended side effects with potentially devastating repercussions. For example, disabling one gene may lead to an increased risk of a different serious illness. Yet some argue that the potential benefits justify the risks. In theory, genetically modifying embryos could give doctors the power to prevent certain inherited diseases before a child is even born.

Promise and Peril

Scientists don't yet have the means to perform such procedures, but research on gene manipulation is progressing so rapidly that experts say that it's only a matter of time before embryo editing techniques are perfected. "Once a game-changing technology is unleashed on the world, it is impossible to contain it," Doudna and Sternberg say.[57]

> **"Once a game-changing technology is unleashed on the world, it is impossible to contain it."[57]**
>
> *– Jennifer Doudna and Samuel Sternberg, biochemists*

Critics worry that advances in genetic engineering will set us on a slippery slope. The same technology used to fix faulty genes that cause diseases could theoretically be used to enhance or upgrade normal genes too. In the future, those with wealth and resources could potentially tinker with their unborn children's DNA to endow them with greater strength or cognitive abilities or to select for physical characteristics such as hair and eye color. This could fuel new forms of social inequality and discrimination, raising ethical concerns about power and privilege.

Genome editing tools offer great promise but also perils. How society will respond to these new technologies in the future remains to be seen. One thing, however, is beyond doubt: advances in genomics will continue to transform medicine in unprecedented ways, with profound implications for human health and well-being. The science of the human genome is making it possible to shape our own genetic destiny to a greater degree than ever before. That power calls for careful oversight and a sense of shared responsibility. "Few technologies are inherently good or bad; what matters is how we use them," Doudna and Sternberg say. "The power to control our species is awesome and terrifying. Deciding how to handle it may be the biggest challenge we have ever faced."[58]

From space exploration to communications to medicine, science and technology have undergone rapid change in the first few decades of the twenty-first century. Sophisticated space probes have taught us about distant worlds and helped us understand Earth's place in the universe. Smartphones have put powerful computers and communications devices in the palms of our hands, and the internet has connected billions of people around the globe. Smart devices hold the promise of making our homes smarter and more efficient, and medical breakthroughs are leading to a better quality of life. As society builds upon these advances, science and technology will continue to push the boundaries of human knowledge.

SOURCE NOTES

Introduction: A Journey of Discovery

1. Quoted in Irene Klotz, "Shuttle Lifts Off on Final Repair Mission to Hubble," *Reuters*, May 10, 2019. www.reuters.com.

2. Quoted in Marcia Dunn, "Last Reach for the Stars," *Times Union*, February 25, 2011. www.timesunion.com.

3. Quoted in Jonathan O'Callaghan, "15 Years of the ISS: The Past, Present, and Future of the Space Station," *Space Answers*, November 20, 2013. www.spaceanswers.com.

4. Quoted in Richard Hollingham, "How the Most Expensive Structure in the World Was Built," *BBC News*, December 21, 2015. www.bbc.com.

5. Quoted in O'Callaghan, "15 Years of the ISS."

6. Jennifer A. Doudna and Samuel H. Sternberg, *A Crack in Creation: Gene Editing and the Unthinkable Power to Control Evolution*. New York: Houghton Mifflin Harcourt, 2017. p. 329.

Chapter 1: What Breakthroughs Are Happening in Space Science?

7. Quoted in "Physicists Announce the Detection of Gravitational Waves," *YouTube - Gizmodo*, February 11, 2016. www.youtube.com.

8. Quoted in Dennis Overbye, "2017 Nobel Prize in Physics Awarded to LIGO Black Hole Researchers," *New York Times*, October 3, 2017. www.nytimes.com.

9. Quoted in Calla Cofield, "Gravitational Waves: What Their Discovery Means for Science and Humanity," *Space*, February 12, 2016. www.space.com.

10. Quoted in Lauren Biron, "LIGO Sees Gravitational Waves," *Symmetry Magazine*, February 11, 2016. www.symmetrymagazine.org.

11. "Gravitational Waves: Why Detect Them?" *LIGO*, n.d. www.ligo.caltech.edu.

12. Quoted in Cofield, "Gravitational Waves."

13. Quoted in Kimberly M.S. Cartier, "The Kepler Revolution," *EOS: Earth and Space Science News*, August 1, 2018. https://eos.org.

14. Nadia Drake, "Famed Planet-Hunting Spacecraft Is Dead. Now What?" *National Geographic*, October 30, 2018. www.nationalgeographic.com.

15. Quoted in Drake, "Famed Planet-Hunting Spacecraft Is Dead."

16. Alan Stern and David Grinspoon, *Chasing New Horizons: Inside the Epic First Mission to Pluto*. New York: Picador, 2018. p. 272.

17. Quoted in Nancy Atkinson, *Incredible Stories from Space: A Behind-the Scenes Look at the Missions Changing Our View of the Cosmos*. Salem, MA: Page Street Publishing, 2016. p. 12.

18. Stern and Grinspoon, *Chasing New Horizons*, p. 187.

19. Quoted in "Looking Back at the 'Year of Pluto,'" *Johns Hopkins Applied Physics Laboratory*, December 31, 2015. http://pluto.jhuapl.edu.

20. Quoted in Atkinson, *Incredible Stories from Space*, p. 28.

21. Quoted in Richard A. Lovett, "To Ultima Thule! What NASA's New Horizons Has Planned for the Holiday Season," *Cosmos*, September 21, 2018. https://cosmosmagazine.com.

Chapter 2: How Has Technology Changed the Way We Communicate?

22. Quoted in Nupur Choudhury, "World Wide Web and Its Journey from Web 1.0 to Web 4.0," *International Journal of Computer Science and Information Technologies* 5, no. 6 (2014): 8096–8100.

23. Ray Girard, Facebook post. November 26, 2018, 9:09 pm.

24. "Facebook's Letter from Mark Zuckerberg—Full Text," *Guardian*, February 1, 2012. www.theguardian.com.

25. Brian McCullough, *How the Internet Happened: From Netscape to the iPhone*. New York: W.W. Norton, 2018. p. 293.

26. David Kirkpatrick, *The Facebook Effect: The Inside Story of the Company That Is Connecting the World*. New York: Simon and Schuster, 2011. p. 15.

27. Farhad Manjoo, "Facebook News Feed Changed Everything," *Slate*, September 12, 2013. www.slate.com.

28. McCullough, *How the Internet Happened*, p. 294.

29. Quoted in McCullough, *How the Internet Happened*, p. 315.

30. Quoted in Casey Phillips, "How Smartphones Revolutionized Society in Less Than a Decade," *Government Technology*, November 20, 2014. www.govtech.com.

31. Quoted in Elizabeth MacBride, "Is Social Media the Tobacco Industry of the 21st Century?" *Forbes*, December 31, 2017. www.forbes.com.

32. Quoted in Sean Illing, "How We're Becoming Slaves to Technology, Explained by an MIT Sociologist," *Vox*, March 27, 2018. www.vox.com.

33. Quoted in John D. Sutter, "How Smartphones Make Us Superhuman," *CNN*, September 10, 2012. www.cnn.com.

34. Quoted in Denis Campbell, "Depression in Girls Linked to Higher Use of Social Media," *Guardian*, January 4, 2019. www.theguardian.com.

35. Quoted in Campbell, "Depression in Girls Linked to Higher Use of Social Media."

Chapter 3: How Have Digital Devices Changed Daily Life?

36. Samuel Greengard, *The Internet of Things*. Cambridge, MA: MIT Press, 2015. p. xviii.

37. Martin Dylan, "The 10 Coolest New Smart Devices of 2018," *CRN*, December 14, 2018. www.crn.com.

38. Quoted in Sonia Rao, "In Today's Homes, Consumers Are Willing to Sacrifice Privacy for Convenience," *Washington Post*, September 11, 2018. www.washingtonpost.com.

39. Kent Dickson, "Why the Smart Home Will Become the Next Major App Platform," *Forbes*, November 19, 2018. www.forbes.com.

40. Quoted in Kelvin Claveria, "Meet Kevin Ashton, the Visionary Technologist Who Named the Internet of Things," *Vision Critical*, March 9, 2019. www.visioncritical.com.

41. Quoted in "HNTB Survey: Americans Expect Self-Driving Vehicles to Be Commonplace Within 15 Years," *HNTB*, June 4, 2018. www.hntb.com.

42. Quoted in Steven Greenhouse, "Driverless Future?" *American Prospect*, March 21, 2017. www.prospect.org.

43. Quoted in Dom Galeon, "Ray Kurzweil: 'AI Will Not Displace Humans, It's Going to Enhance Us,'" *Futurism*, November 7, 2017. www.futurism.com.

Chapter 4: How Are Medical Advances Improving Lives?

44. Jane Wakefield, "TED 2014: Meeting the Real Bionic Man," *BBC News*, March 20, 2014. www.bbc.com.

45. Quoted in "Hand That Sees Offers New Hope to Amputees," *Newcastle University Press Office*, May 3, 2017. www.ncl.ac.uk.

46. Quoted in "Hand That Sees Offers New Hope to Amputees."

47. Quoted in John Hamilton, "Paralyzed Man Uses Thoughts to Control His Own Arm and Hand," *NPR News*, March 28, 2017. www.npr.org.

48. Quoted in "'Groundbreaking' Technology Restores Movement in Paralyzed Man," *CBS News*, March 29, 2017. www.cbsnews.com.

49. Quoted in David Cox, "The MIT Professor Obsessed with Building Intelligent Prosthetics," *Motherboard*, June 20, 2016. https://motherboard.vice.com.

50. Quoted in Mark Piesing, "Medical Robotics: Would You Trust a Robot with a Scalpel," *Guardian*, October 10, 2014. www.theguardian.com.

51. Quoted in Taylor Kubota, "Deep Learning Algorithm Does as Well as Dermatologists in Identifying Skin Cancer," *Stanford News*, January 1, 2017. https://news.stanford.edu.

52. Quoted in "The Human Genome Project Completion: Frequently Asked Questions," *National Human Genome Research Institute*, n.d. www.genome.gov.

53. Quoted in Lauren Dunn and Maggie Fox, "This New Cancer Drug Goes Straight to the Cause of the Cancer," *NBC News*, November 27, 2018. www.nbcnews.com.

54. Quoted in James Gallagher, "'Designer Cells' Reverse One-Year-Old's Cancer," *BBC News*, November 5, 2015. www.bbc.com.

55. Quoted in Sharon Begley, "Claim of CRISPR'd Baby Girls Stuns Genome Editing Summit," *STAT News*, November 26, 2018. www.statnews.com.

56. Quoted in Suzanne Sataline, "Scientist in China Defends Human Embryo Gene Editing," *Guardian*, November 28, 2018. www.theguardian.com.

57. Doudna and Sternberg, *A Crack in Creation*, p. 239.

58. Doudna and Sternberg, *A Crack in Creation*, p. 240.

FOR FURTHER RESEARCH

Books

Toney Allman, *Cutting Edge Medical Technology*. San Diego, CA: ReferencePoint Press, 2017.

Toney Allman, *Genetics and Medicine*. San Diego, CA: ReferencePoint Press, 2018.

Richard Gaughan, *Gravitational Waves Explained*. New York: Enslow Publishing, 2019.

Martin Jenkins, *Exploring Space: From Galileo to the Mars Rover and Beyond*. Somerville, MA: Candlewick Press, 2017.

Karen Latchana Kenney, *Exoplanets: Worlds Beyond Our Solar System*. Minneapolis, MN: Twenty-First Century Books, 2017.

Stephanie Sammartino McPherson, *Artificial Intelligence: Building Smarter Machines*. Minneapolis, MN: Twenty-First Century Books, 2018.

Bradley Steffens, *Cutting Edge Internet Technology*. San Diego, CA: ReferencePoint Press, 2017.

Internet Sources

Lauren Biron, "LIGO Sees Gravitational Waves," *Symmetry Magazine*, February 11, 2016. www.symmetrymagazine.org.

David Cox, "The MIT Professor Obsessed with Building Intelligent Prosthetics," *Motherboard*, June 20, 2016. http://motherboard.vice.com.

Nadia Drake, "A NASA Telescope Just Doubled Its Haul of Known Planets," *National Geographic*, May 10, 2016. http://news.nationalgeographic.com.

Kevin Drum, "You Will Lose Your Job to a Robot—and Sooner Than You Think," *Mother Jones*, November/December 2017. www.motherjones.com.

Bree Fowler, "Gifts That Snoop? The Internet of Things Is Wrapped in Privacy Concerns," *Consumer Reports*, December 13, 2017. www.consumerreports.org.

James Gallagher, "Dawn of Gene-Editing Medicine?" *BBC News*, November 6, 2015. www.bbc.com.

Websites

NASA Student Portal
www.nasa.gov/audience/forstudents/index.html
NASA's portal for students has a wealth of resources on space science, including informational articles, videos, photos, and listings of educational programs and opportunities.

National Human Genome Research Institute Student Page
www.genome.gov/students/
The National Human Genome Research Institute directed the US contribution to the Human Genome Project. Its page for students is a clearinghouse of information about the project and about human genetics.

Planet Hunters
www.zooniverse.org/projects/nora-dot-eisner/planet-hunters-tess
Planet Hunters is a project that allows volunteer citizen scientists to check data from the Transiting Exoplanet Survey Satellite (TESS) to help detect patterns of starlight that might indicate a planetary system outside of our solar system. The website also includes a discussion forum and informational resources on exoplanets.

INDEX

INDEX CONTINUED

IMAGE CREDITS

ABOUT THE AUTHOR

Elisabeth Herschbach is an editor and writer from Washington, DC.